ANDREW LLOYD WEBBER

GOLD

A REALLY USEFUL GROUP PUBLICATION

WWW.REALLYUSEFUL.COM

EXCLUSIVE DISTRIBUTORS:
MUSIC SALES LIMITED
14-15 BERNERS STREET, LONDON W1T 3LJ, UK.
MUSIC SALES PTY LIMITED
120 ROTHSCHILD AVENUE, ROSEBERY, NSW 2018, AUSTRALIA.

WWW.MUSICSALES.COM

ORDER NO. RG10505
ISBN 978-1-84772-302-4

  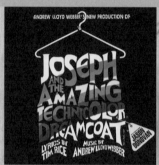  

MUSIC PROCESSED BY DAKOTA MUSIC SERVICE.
COVER ARTWORK COURTESY OF REALLY USEFUL RECORDS.

PRINTED IN THE EU.

YOUR GUARANTEE OF QUALITY:
AS PUBLISHERS, WE STRIVE TO PRODUCE EVERY BOOK TO THE HIGHEST
COMMERCIAL STANDARDS. WHILE ENDEAVOURING TO RETAIN THE
ORIGINAL RUNNING ORDER OF THE RECORDED ALBUM, THE BOOK HAS BEEN
CAREFULLY DESIGNED TO MINIMISE AWKWARD PAGE TURNS AND TO MAKE
PLAYING FROM IT A REAL PLEASURE. PARTICULAR CARE HAS BEEN GIVEN TO
SPECIFYING ACID-FREE, NEUTRAL-SIZED PAPER MADE FROM PULPS WHICH
HAVE NOT BEEN ELEMENTAL CHLORINE BLEACHED. THIS PULP IS
FROM FARMED SUSTAINABLE FORESTS AND WAS PRODUCED WITH SPECIAL
REGARD FOR THE ENVIRONMENT. THROUGHOUT, THE PRINTING AND
BINDING HAVE BEEN PLANNED TO ENSURE A STURDY, ATTRACTIVE PUBLICATION
WHICH SHOULD GIVE YEARS OF ENJOYMENT. IF YOUR COPY FAILS TO MEET
OUR HIGH STANDARDS, PLEASE INFORM US AND WE WILL GLADLY REPLACE IT.

A REALLY USEFUL GROUP PUBLICATION
WWW.REALLYUSEFUL.COM

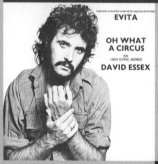

JESUS CHRIST
SUPER STAR

EVITA

Song & Dance

CATS

REQUIEM

The
PHANTOM
of the
OPERA

Aspects of Love

JOSEPH
AND THE
AMAZING
TECHNICOLOR
DREAMCOAT

SUNSET BLVD.

WHISTLE
DOWN THE
WIND

THE
WOMAN
IN
WHITE

SUPERSTAR

MUSIC BY ANDREW LLOYD WEBBER
LYRICS BY TIM RICE

Ev - 'ry time I look at you I
Tell me what you think a - bout your

don't un - der - stand,—
friends at the top,—

why you let the things you did get
who d'you think be - sides your - self's the

9

I DON'T KNOW HOW TO LOVE HIM

MUSIC BY ANDREW LLOYD WEBBER
LYRICS BY TIM RICE

Slowly, tenderly and very expressively

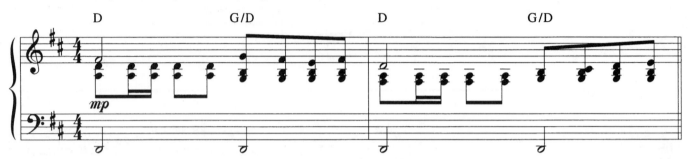

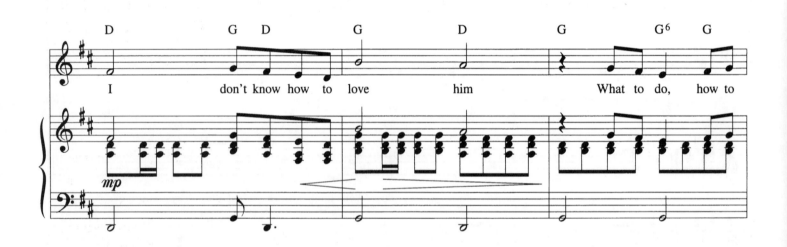

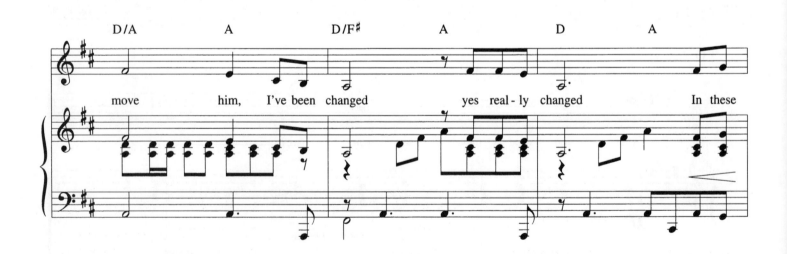

DON'T CRY FOR ME ARGENTINA

MUSIC BY ANDREW LLOYD WEBBER
LYRICS BY TIM RICE

It won't be ea - sy, you'll think it strange when I

time, I love you and hope you love me.

Don't cry for me Ar - gen - ti - na. Mm

Don't cry for me Ar - gen -

ti - na, _____ the truth is I ne - ver left you. All through my

wild days, _____ my mad ex - is - tence, I kept my pro - mise, don't keep your

dis - tance. _____ Have I said too much, there's no - thing more I can think of to

say to you. _____ But all you have to do is

look at me to know that ev - 'ry word is true. ⌣

ANOTHER SUITCASE IN ANOTHER HALL

MUSIC BY ANDREW LLOYD WEBBER
LYRICS BY TIM RICE

don't ex - pect my love af - fairs to last for long, ne - ver
time and time a - gain I've said that I don't care that I'm im-
call in three months time and I'll be fine I know well

fool my - self that my dreams _____ will come true.
mune to self gloom, that I'm hard _____ through and through but
may - be not that fine but I'll sur - vive _____ an - y how, I

Be - ing used to trou - ble I an - ti - - - ci - pate it but
ev - ery time it mat - ters all my words de - sert me so
won't re - call the names and plac - es of this sad oc - ca - sion, but

all the same I hate it would - n't you, so what hap - pens
an - y - one can hurt me, and they do, so what hap - pens
that's no con - so - la - tion here and now, so what hap - pens

now, so what hap - pens now? Where am I

CHOIR

An - oth - er suit - case in an - oth - er hall, — take your pic - ture off an - oth - er wall. —

OH WHAT A CIRCUS

MUSIC BY ANDREW LLOYD WEBBER
LYRICS BY TIM RICE

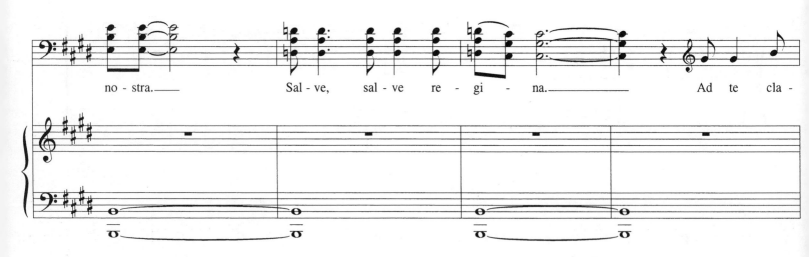

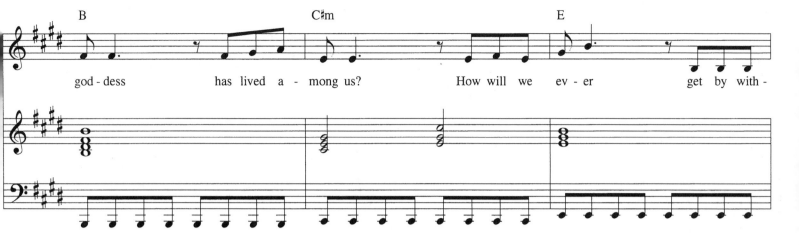

god - dess   has lived a - mong us?   How will we ev - er   get by with -

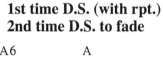

1st time D.S. (with rpt.)
2nd time D.S. to fade

out   her?

Verse 2

Oh, what an exit! That's how to go!
When they're ringing your curtain down
Demand to be buried like Eva Peron.
It's quite a sunset
And good for the country in a roundabout way
We've made the front pages of all the world's papers today!

Verse 3

Salve regina, mater misericordiae,
Vita dulcedo et spes nostra.
Salve, salve regina,
Ad te clamamus exules filii Eva,
Ad te suspiramus gementes et flentes
O clemens, O pia!

Verse 4

She had her moments, she had some style.
The best show in town was the crowd
Outside the Casa Rosada crying "Eva Peron".
But that's all gone now
As soon as the smoke from the funeral clears
We're all going to see - and how! - she did nothing for years.
You let down your people Evita
You were supposed to have been immortal
That's all they wanted
Not much to ask for
But in the end you could not deliver.

Verse 5

Salve regina, mater misericordiae,
Vita dulcedo et spes nostra.
Salve, salve regina,
Ad te clamamus exules filii Eva,
Ad te suspiramus gementes et flentes
O clemens, O pia! (Repeat)

TAKE THAT LOOK OFF YOUR FACE

MUSIC BY ANDREW LLOYD WEBBER
LYRICS BY DON BLACK

MEMORY

MUSIC BY ANDREW LLOYD WEBBER
LYRICS BY TREVOR NUNN AFTER T.S. ELIOT

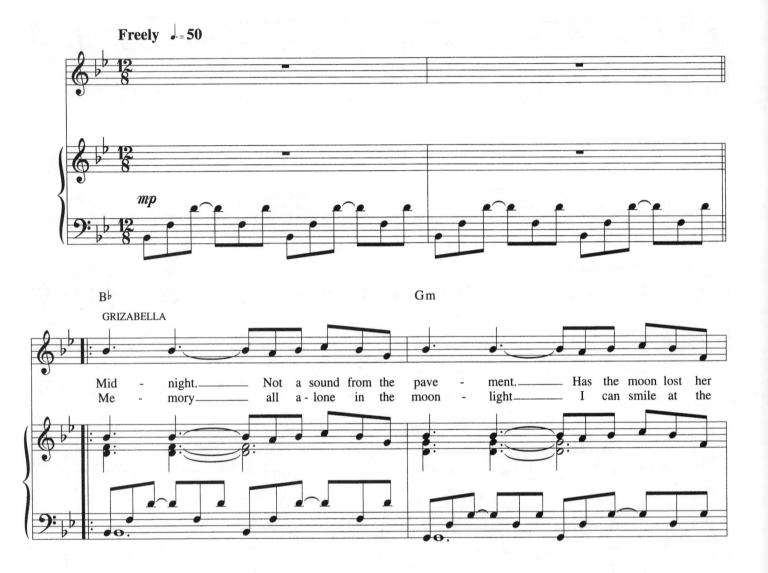

Burnt out ends of smo - ky days,—— the

stale cold smell—— of morn - ing.—— The street lamp dies, an - oth - er

night is ov - er,—— an - oth - er day is dawn - ing.——

40

PIE JESU

MUSIC BY ANDREW LLOYD WEBBER

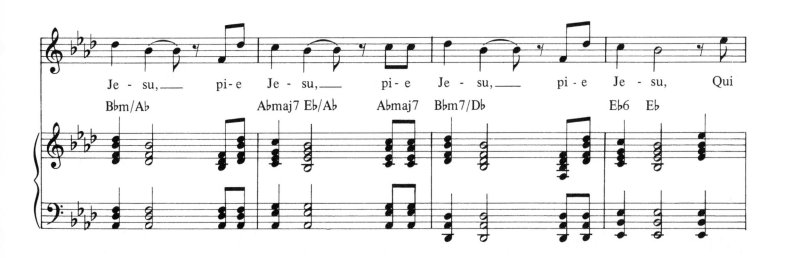

re-qui-em.

SOLO BOY *mp*

Pi - e Je - su,____ pi - e Je - su,____ pi - e

Ab   Bbm/Ab   Eb7/Ab   Ab

Qui tol - lis pec -ca - ta mun-di,

Je - su,____ pi - e Je - su,   Qui tol - lis pec -ca - ta mun-di,

SOPRANO   *p*

ALTO

*Hm*____

TENOR

BASS

p

Bbm7/Db   Eb7   Db   Eb

44

THE PHANTOM OF THE OPERA

MUSIC BY ANDREW LLOYD WEBBER
LYRICS BY CHARLES HART
ADDITIONAL LYRICS BY RICHARD STILGOE & MIKE BATT

47

The Phan - tom of the Op - e - ra is now ____ your/my mas - ter mind.

PHANTOM: Sing my angel of music

KRISTIN: He's there, the Phan - tom of the Op - e - ra. ____ Ah.

PHANTOM: Sing once again with me our strange duet; my power over you

PHANTOM: *Continue over Fade*

The Phantom of the Opera
Is now your mastermind;
I am here
Inside your mind.
I am everywhere,
You're in my power.
Sing,
Sing, my angel of music,
Sing. . . .

ALL I ASK OF YOU

MUSIC BY ANDREW LLOYD WEBBER
LYRICS BY CHARLES HART
ADDITIONAL LYRICS BY RICHARD STILGOE

Say you need me with you, here be - side you, an - y - where you go, let me go too.

Christ - ine, __ that's all I ask of you.

CHRISTINE

Say you'll share with me one love, one life - time; say the word and I will fol - low you. __

TOGETHER

Share each day with me, each night, each morn - ing. Say you love me!

CHRISTINE

RAOUL

You know I

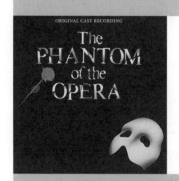

THE MUSIC OF THE NIGHT

MUSIC BY ANDREW LLOYD WEBBER
LYRICS BY CHARLES HART
ADDITIONAL LYRICS BY RICHARD STILGOE

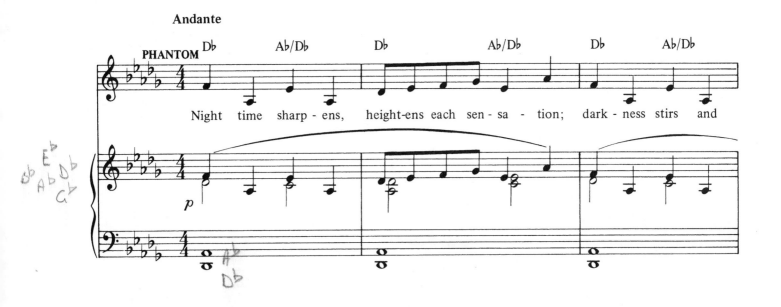

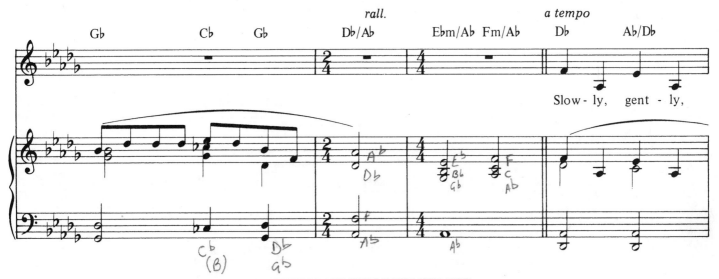

eyes let your spi-rit start to soar and you'll live as you've nev-er lived be-fore.

Soft-ly, deft-ly, mu-sic shall ca-ress you. Hear it, feel it,

se-cret-ly po-ssess you. O-pen up your mind let your fan-ta-sies un-wind in this

dark-ness which you know you can-not fight, the dark-ness of the mu-sic of the

LOVE CHANGES EVERYTHING

MUSIC BY ANDREW LLOYD WEBBER
LYRICS BY DON BLACK & CHARLES HART

Off _____ in- to the world we go, plan- ning fu- tures, shap- ing years.

Love _____ bursts in and sud- den- ly, all our wis- dom dis- ap- pears.

Love _____ makes fools of ev- ery- one: all the rules we make are

ANY DREAM WILL DO

MUSIC BY ANDREW LLOYD WEBBER
LYRICS BY TIM RICE

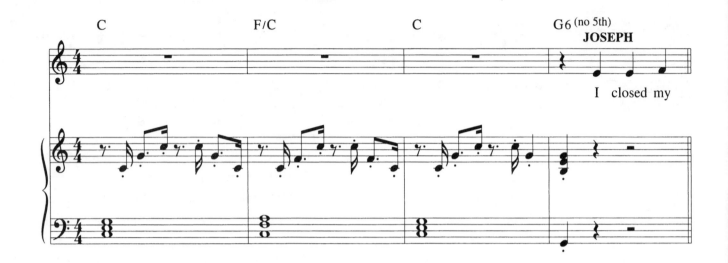

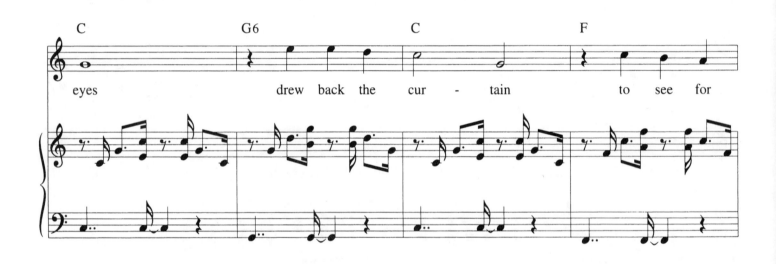

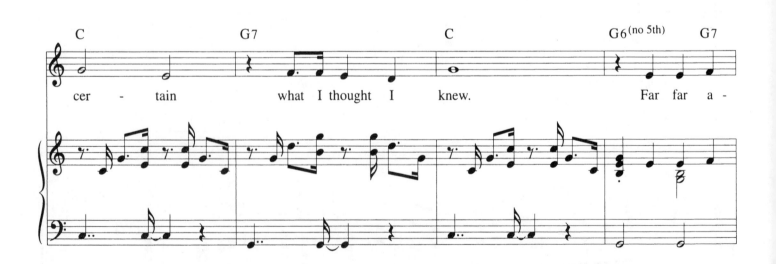

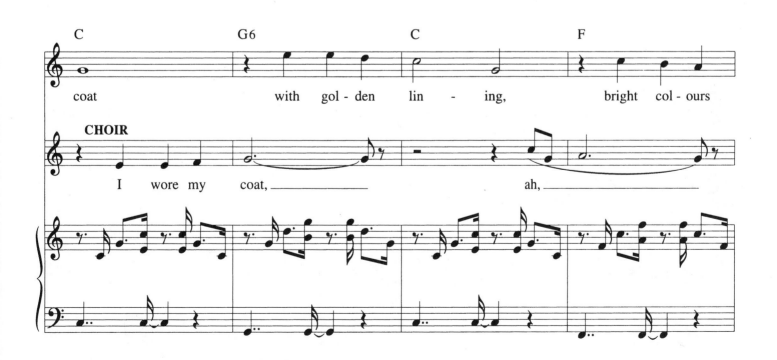

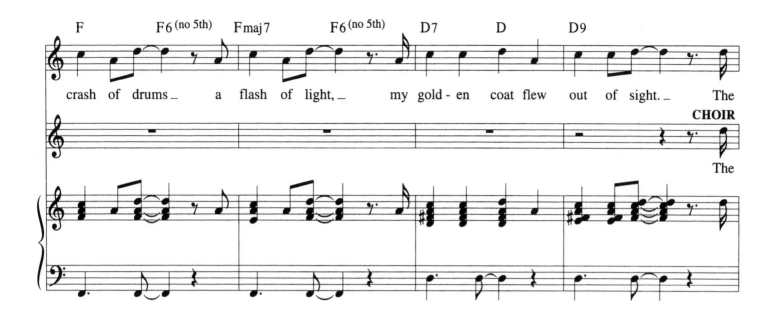

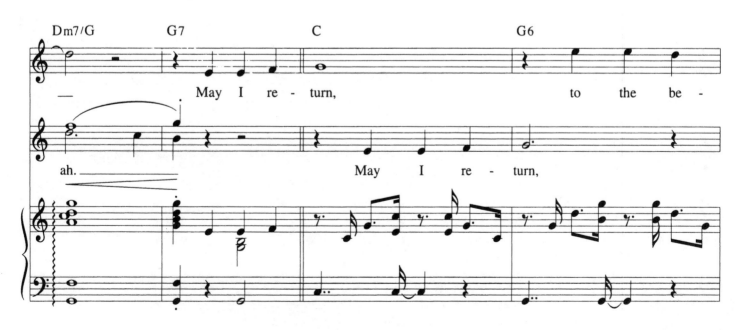

gin - ning, the light is dim - ming and the dream is

ah, _____ ah. _____

too, the world and I, we are still

The world and I, _____

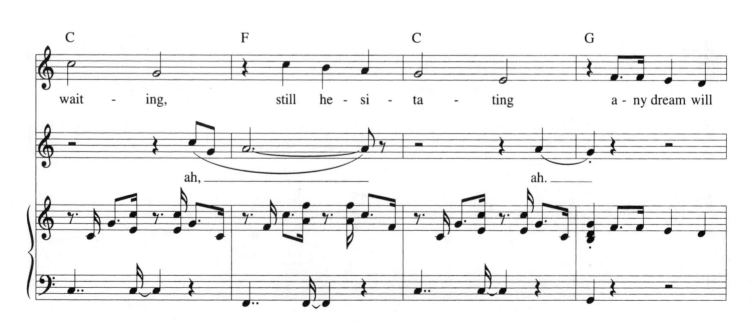

wait - ing, still he - si - ta - ting a - ny dream will

ah, _____ ah. _____

AMIGOS PARA SIEMPRE
(FRIENDS FOR LIFE)

MUSIC BY ANDREW LLOYD WEBBER
LYRICS BY DON BLACK

life not just a sum-mer or a spring A - MI - GOS PA - RA SIEM - PRE.

THE PERFECT YEAR

MUSIC BY ANDREW LLOYD WEBBER
LYRICS BY DON BLACK & CHRISTOPHER HAMPTON

ev-ery-thing I want is here, if you're with me,_____ next year will be_____ the per-fect

year. Be-fore we play_____ some dan-ger-ous game,_____ be-fore we fan_____ some harm-less

flame, we have to ask_____ if this is wise,_____ and if the game_____ is worth the

prize. With this wine, and with this mu - sic, how can a - ny-thing be

clear? Let's wait and see,_____ it may just be_____ the per-fect year.

NORMA

It's New Year's Eve, and hopes are high, dance one year

in, kiss one good - bye, an - oth - er chance, an - oth - er start, so ma - ny

AS IF WE NEVER SAID GOODBYE

MUSIC BY ANDREW LLOYD WEBBER
LYRICS BY DON BLACK & CHRISTOPHER HAMPTON
WITH CONTRIBUTIONS BY AMY POWERS

al - ways._____ We'll have ear-ly morn-ing mad - ness,_____ we'll have

ma-gic in the mak - ing,_____ yes, ev-ery-thing's as if we ne - ver said good -

- bye,_____ yes, ev-ery-thing's as if we ne - ver said good - bye._____

We taught the world new ways to dream.

YOU MUST LOVE ME

MUSIC BY ANDREW LLOYD WEBBER
LYRICS BY TIM RICE

Cer - tain - ties   disappear   *(2º see block lyric)*

what do we do_____ for our dream to sur - vive,

how do we keep_____ all our pas - sions a - live as we used to do?_____

_____ Deep in my heart I'm con - ceal - ing

2° lyric
Why are you at my side?
How can I be any use to you now?
Give me a chance and I'll let you see how
Nothing has changed.
Deep in my heart I'm concealing
Things that I'm longing to say,
Scared to confess what I'm feeling
Frightened you'll slip away,
You must love me.

WHISTLE DOWN THE WIND

MUSIC BY ANDREW LLOYD WEBBER
LYRICS BY JIM STEINMAN

I'll be there to hold you, I'll be there to stop the chills and all the weep- ing.___ Make it

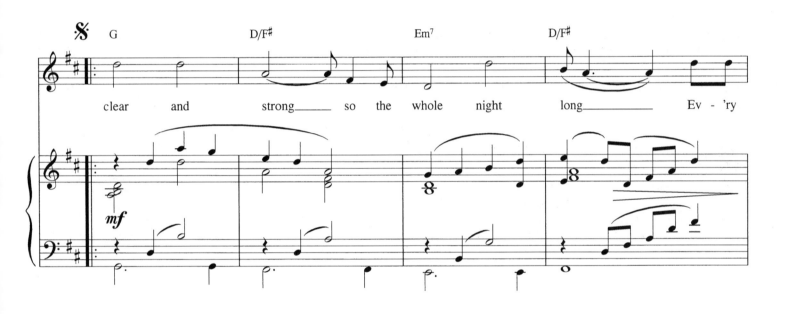

clear and strong___ so the whole night long___ Ev - 'ry

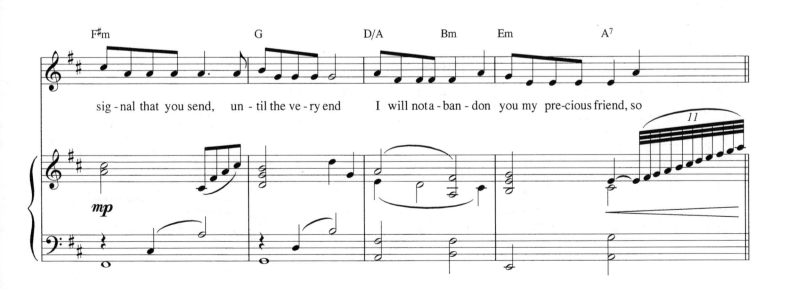

sig - nal that you send, un - til the ve - ry end I will not a - ban - don you my pre-cious friend, so

try and stem the tide_____ then you'll raise a ban - ner_____ send a

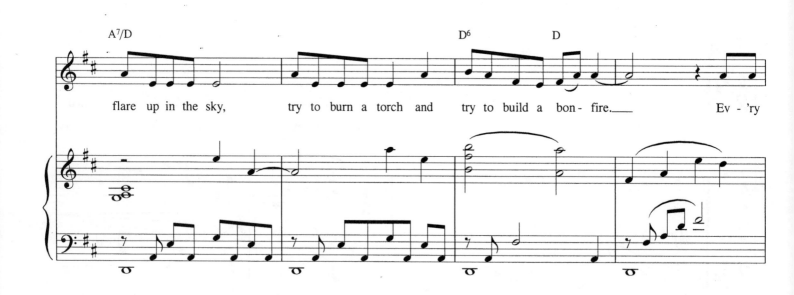

flare up in the sky, try to burn a torch and try to build a bon - fire.___ Ev - 'ry

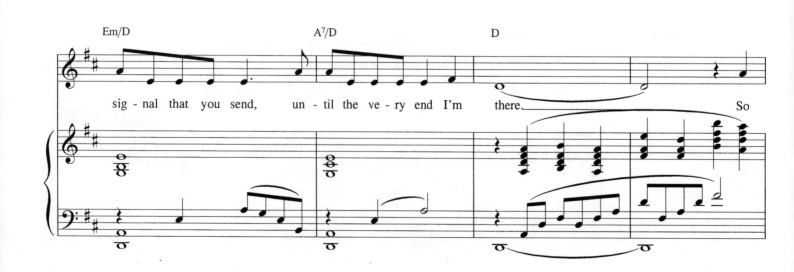

sig - nal that you send, un - til the ve - ry end I'm there.___ So

whis - tle down the wind for I have al ways been right here.

(1.)

Make it

whis - tle down the wind for I have al - ways been right there.

NO MATTER WHAT

MUSIC BY ANDREW LLOYD WEBBER
LYRICS BY JIM STEINMAN

No mat-ter what they tell us, no mat-ter what they do,
If on-ly tears were laugh-ter, if on-ly night was day,

no mat-ter what they teach us, what we be-lieve is true.
if on-ly prayers were an-swered then we would hear God say.

I BELIEVE MY HEART

MUSIC BY ANDREW LLOYD WEBBER
LYRICS BY DAVID ZIPPEL

When-ev-er I see your face___ the world dis-ap-pears.

All in a sin-gle glance so re-veal - ing.

123456789